You're DEER-lightful
in every way,
making every day
like Valentine's Day.

You are my
PURR-fect match.
You make my
heart go POUNCE.

Roses are red,
violets are blue.
You're FOX-cinating,
I love you!

You're 'NUT' just
my Valentine,
you're the love of
my life!

You make my heart
skip a 'SQUEAK!.

My love for you is as
big as a turkey's
GOBBLE-GOBBLE!

'PECK'a boo!
I see my Valentine,
and it is you!

I love you
more than honey.
You're un-BEAR-lievably
special, my Valentine!

You are my
·TWEET·-heart.
You make my
heart flutter.

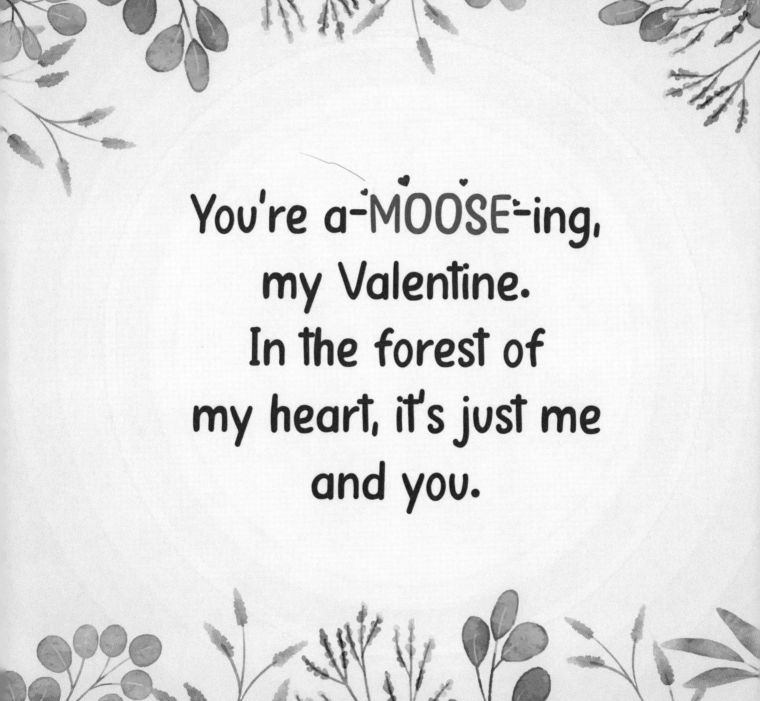

You're a-MOOSE-ing,
my Valentine.
In the forest of
my heart, it's just me
and you.

You are the OTTER
half of my soul.
I am incomplete
without you.

HOPPY Valentine's Day!
Our love will never
stop hopping along.

With you,
every day is a
HOWL-iday of love!

You are my
favorite BANDIT.
You stole my heart
in a minute.

WHOO's my Valentine?
It's you, OWL-ways so
wise and true.

Made in the USA
Las Vegas, NV
25 September 2024

95749238R00024